LOVE DRUNK

By: Scott Antwan

I dedicate this book to

Doris M. Evans

"Thank you for proving the loyalty of

love. You are my example of what

pure, unadulterated, devoted,

unconditional love should resemble

and for that I appreciate and revere

you."

Love your Grandson, - Scott

Sincere heartfelt thanks to my guardian

angels -

Gone but never forgotten:

John Buchan

Shirley Evans

Ruth Miller

Lottie Baker

Kimberly K. Hughes

Kenneth "KC" Shaw

"I can feel all of you watching over

me."

Special thanks for the amazing cover
art go to the graphic design team of

Ink Mind, LLC

Contact @ InkMind.com

Love
Drunk

Table for one

From the back of my think box
Many answers are sought
As the venom of my visions
-jabs to heckle
-jabs to haunt
While the truth is bled
Saying that I caused myself this pain
Telling that I wished myself this stain
But how?
It's only love I seek
Though tempted to give in to the bleak
I fight my own quest
Failing every test
I am lost in this sadness that is alone
Alone
Just me
Table for one

Love is a splendidly cunning
conundrum

Chapter One

We enter this life alone
Searching for someone to
belong

Have Not

I speak in love
Heard love I've not

I dream in love
Taste love I've not

I wish in love
Had love I've not

I crave in love
Felt love I've not

I hope in love
Waste love I've not

I believe in love
Curse love I've not

I wait in love
Chase love I've not

Joy

Can you hear my song?
Thump of my heart beats the sounds of
Oooh ahh oooh ahh oooooh
All because of you
My song now has lyrics that live
-and meanings that give
My heart is chasing yours
Beating so fast, that it has beaten past me
-and went straight to you
I wonder if you hear it calling you
I wonder if you feel it chasing you
I wonder if you know that it is just for you
That my heart plays its remix
In my dance I am lost to the notes of true happiness
It's evaded me so long
That I figured I was wrong
For *Love*
We've played this game of omitting my name
But *Love* please see me
Peek-a-boo I see you
Though you're looking through and past me
Maybe I'm nothing
Nothing that *Love* would want to consort with
I've drawn a path to my conscience
Yet *Love* has still passed me by
Sketched a ring around my soul
Yet cupid chose different targets
I watch them smile after impact
While I sit and await my turn
Wishing for an arrow to pierce me
Hoping for a cherub to choose me
Praying for *Love* to like me
My loneliness has taken over with authority all of my
prayers
-and hollowed my hopes

For at this time I am numb
Waiting to be set in action by romance
This yearning leaving gaps in my person the size of
courtships
An open space
For a chosen face
Vacancy springs eternal
Leaving me sitting here
Key in hand
Lock unlocked
Pleading with *Love* to look my way
Begging my beacon to beckon **Joy**

Midnight Star

How bright do I have to shine for you to notice my
glow?
I'm even blinking
Hoping that you catch my sequence
But nothing –
From what I can see
You're the type that I would love to wish on
Wishing that you would wish for me
My brightness is too bright for most
While my height is out of reach for others
But for you I will dim and dip
Until I am ground in your grip
I look at you and see myself
A lonely star
Coasting the cosmos
Looking to belong to someone
Praying that my show will pay off
But nothing –
Catch me before I burn out
And my light is gone forever
Catch me before I am morphed into black
And my shine is nil
Catch me if you can
I'm trying to help you

Without Reason

Without reason
My heart invites your pain
And welcomes your invasion
Knowing that the truth proves loneliness
While the night cries promises of love eternal
Though you don't even know your felony
Each blink, each wink shuts the door to happiness
While the flood gates of ill spill secrets and sorrows
My heart is full of you
And void of the know how to lock you out
Your smile seals my cozy coffin
Hammered shut with visions of us inseparable
Though my reality is blue
For when I knew how
I knew better
Than to wish the hoax of love

From a distance

From a distance I watched you dance through life
without a partner
Spinning recklessly with glee
While wishing that your partner was me
From a distance I felt my quest for bliss was ending
As my search for me began
Tick-tock of time
Doesn't help my mind
While counting the days until you are mine
From a distance I watched my destiny dance
-beneath the moon
Tracing my heart
With every move
Swirling circles around my essence
Spitting secrets on my fire
From a distance I fell in love

I see visions staring

I'm standing and I'm still
The stare of eyes I feel
Have froze me in time
True sensations sublime
In the stillness I hide
Choking on my pride
For they see me
My mask is ailed
Its task it failed
My weakness is open
My strengths are now broken
This stare is strong
This gaze is long
For they see me
A lifetime of hiding
In one moment I'm caught
Your discovery I'm fighting
Have you found what you sought?
For they see me
Seen Enough?
Anymore to find?
Think you're tough?
Then read my mind
For then you'll see me
You're trying too hard
My will you won't crack
I'm holding your card
Is it red?
Is it black?
I can tell you for sure
That you are trapped in a trap
I can promise from here
That there is no turning back
In this gaze you have locked on me
Locked and loaded, my conscience imploded

Loaded and cocked, my resistance is blocked
This is a glare
That is stripping me bare
Armorless and naked
Powerless and vacant
Never has my core been exposed
For yours and forsaken
My armor you've taken
I brace for the war you've imposed
Though the first blow you struck was a smile

You looked at me and purpose discovered my heart

Chapter Two

I've got it bad
And that ain't good

Maturing a silent cry for love

I see you over there seeing me
I wonder if we're sharing thoughts
Because at times I hear your mind
While seeing your visions
It scares me to think that we could be one
Though I'm frightened into your arms
While shielding myself from your threat
The threat of love
So deep is my fear
That a voice crowds my ear
Whispering "love is near"
Insisting that I keep you here
Suggesting my heart is sheer
Revealing my feelings are clear
For love has found my sphere
But nothing can erase this fear
Oh Dear!
How I wish I could let go
And grab on to you
But my best battalion battles breaks in my heart
For my fighters fear
That if love creeps in
Pain will begin
And then sorrow will win
Control of my mental

Though in the back of my mind
You can hear anytime
You try
A maturing silent cry for love

A cry that craves your heat
While enjoying your cool
Lonely life lacking love looking lovingly like love lost
Though the game has just begun
On your mark
Get set
Go away
Come back
If you have the knack
To turn my heart from black
I can stop their attack
But if you lack the skill
My fighters will kill
Any hopes and any will
That you thought were real
For they work for free
Protecting me
From tongues like thee
That'll speak my heart free
They'll stab til' you see
That my heart is the key
That unlocks the vault
Though I warn you to halt
For if it's your fault
That my heart's dipped in salt
No mercy shall come your way
For fierce are my fighters
When they deal with defiers
So I hope you're true
Before black and blue
Is your soul and your you

Though in the back of my mind
You can hear anytime
You try
A maturing silent cry for love

Silent is the cry
As it spills from my eye
Tears there but dry
For my fears hold inside
All the pain that I hide
Hence tattooed is my heart
You were doomed from the start
But your fight don't part
My cry is getting louder
For when my eyes are bare
It's your face that I wish there
To give my warriors a scare
When you show them that you care
Because to face them is a dare
So I suggest that you play fair
Or my friend you should beware
You're not the first opponent on the battlefield
But you are the first that I want to win
For I have matured within

Clocked Coward

I find in my mind
That it's fine to pine
Daydreams are never only dreams
For me they are real
Picturing our together
Frame by frame of predicted jubilance
My imaginary my true attention
To pine is to imagine
To pine is to create
To pine is simply to adore
While still in the real I cherish
I believe you are a gift from Zeus
A present just for me
Not to be shared
But to be prized and protected
Made safe from the wrath of the truth
Because if the truth were to reign
You would discover that you are adored from a distance
Being watched and worshiped by a coward
Cowardice causing together time to be lost
Allowing more solo time to be clocked
Afraid of having to let go of imaginary perfection
I play mute
Because my truth is that I am flawed
And could never handle making you flee
Will never survive watching you leave
Can't ever let you go
So I stay stuck struck strictly simply silently adoring you
From a distance
But how I feel is as real as the Sun's heat
Praying for courage to free my imprisoned tongue
For if I were to speak my wishes
Into your perfect ears
Heaven's answers could rain down we
Allowing for my daydreams to cease

So that our game could begin
And our reality could bloom sweeter than my illusions

We kissed beneath the Moon's eye
And *Fantasia* became real

Blue Paradise

The sapphire empire inside your eyes
Sends me sailing
Across the Pacific to be specific
Your crystal blues
Give shades, make hues
That paint the truth of the soul inside
Though behind the cobalt you hide
Is it pain? Or how about pride?
Either or I can't ignore the sense of self that seeps
How it bleeds, how it creeps
From those magic orbs
That scan and absorb
The pace and the peace of the scene at hand
While on principal you stand
Striking a match beneath the fire of my desire
Quenching the questions and quagmires I create
While drowning and drenching
The trials and trenching of fate
I find freedom in the shimmer of your Atlantic
Shedding the shackles of lonely
With eyes for yours only
I am frozen by the arctic pursuit
From your eyes that shoot
Aiming at my guardian wall
Disregarding how old, how tall
For the promise of your passion
Is enough to flood the Sun
On dark days absent of hope
Void of rays, preaching to cope
Now when the Sun is gone
And the sky is gray
I look into your blues
To chase my blues away
For in your eyes
Is my Blue Paradise

Outcast

Your eyes undress me
I don't want cover

Your presence awakens me
I wish to sleep no more

Your warmth boils me
I do not want ice

Your touch degrades me
I feel no shame

Your tenderness drowns me
I shun rescue

Your arms entrap me
I don't search for exits

Your passion chases me
I wait to get caught

Your mind confuses me
I don't want the answer

Your sensuality enslaves me
I run from freedom

Your devotion bewilders me
I don't look for reasons

Your gaze imprisons me
I wish to stay jailed

Your voice weakens me
I am spent

Your hands molest me
I shall never tell

Your courage empowers me
I am invincible

Your aroma excites me
I rest four senses

Your song brings me to life
I lay and play dead

Your compliments feed me
My ego is starved

Your whispers seduce me
I can hear you

Your smile brings the light
I am dark while you sleep

Your laugh keeps me young
I age when you leave

Your charm intoxicates me
I banish sobriety

Your words soothe me
I am forever shaken

Your caress entangles me
I don't want to get loose

Your desires embrace me
I am warm all over

Your joy tickles me
I surrender to glee

Your love poisons me
I invite death

Your emotions capture me
I am a prisoner of war

Your absence kills me
I suffocate in your space

Your sweet nothings rain down on me
I run from shelter

Your appetite beckons my flesh
I do not keep you waiting

Your skin envelops me
I fret my release

Your tongue punishes me
I don't wish to be forgiven

Your lips taunt me
I beg for more

Your limbs possess me
I am eternally yours

Your heart gives me rhythm
I am now on beat

Your body entices me
I have never wanted so

Your soul completes me
I wish to stay undone

Your commitment challenges me
Let the games begin

Your love is forbidden
I welcome exile

Chapter Three

You are my addiction

Narcotic

Ever since you entered my vein
My heart's had a new refrain

I'm high off of you
Inhaling your love
I exhale my glee
If I puff puff pass
I will cease to be

For this is a high I dare not share
Let's get hot and heavy
While the spoon is steady
I'm my own pusher
Choosing addiction over eviction
For this high I've paid the cost
Though it's my sanity that's lost
I will snort you til' my nostrils cave
Until my blood aches from the taste I crave

I'm high off of you
I inhale your love
Exhaling my glee
If I puff puff pass
I will cease to be

You are my gateway to bliss
Once my lips and pipe kiss
Sealing the deal

That makes you real
Is an offer I can't resist
If I must kill, must rob, must steal
For you I will insist

I'm high off of you
Inhaling your love
I exhale my glee
If I puff puff pass
I will cease to be

An overdose
Though sounds morose
Would be the answer to my prayers
Either up my nose
Arm
Needle
Hose
Or laced on paper in squares
You'll be my drug of choice

I'm high off of you
I inhale your love
Exhaling my glee
If I puff puff pass
I will cease

In Patience

I'm lying here on high
And I haven't moved
You did that with one look – one smile
I was in orbit when you walked in the room
You send me to Pluto and back
Can't wait until I reach Uranus
Ignited by your touch
Inflamed by your majesty
Burn me alive
I beg for third degree
Burn me alive
Who taught you to do that?
Thank them for me
I'm lying here on high
And I haven't moved
Except for the quiver in my soul
From the tremble in your voice
Each breath seducing me
Exhaling whispers
I taste your requests
Feed me more
I am starved for you
My appetite is only you
Disregard the menu
One order of heaven, dipped in sauce
Mmm mmm good to the last drop
Licking the bowl
While asking for seconds
I'm lying here on high
And I haven't moved
Patiently awaiting our rematch
I won't lose twice
Unless you want me to
I aim to please

Spellbound

Seems I've been swept by this rapture
While gleefully caught in your capture
Intrigued by the song of your soul
My heart burning hot from cold
My mind paces around possibility
Wanting to know which way to go
Waiting to see what this rapture will be
Though the truth of my quest is bare
Wishing to be caught by Cupid's snare
Hoping my dreams will come to be
Praying this snare traps joy with me
Though fear has me froze
From my fingers, through my toes
Afraid that Cupid is again playing games
Those tricky cherubs can trick you when matching
names
Being tired of the lonely
While hungry for the happy
My yearn for union supersedes my lack of practice
With rhythms set pace by a smile and a kiss
My soul has been sent into the forbidden dance
While waiting to see if it's luck
Or if it's chance
That has sealed our fate
For this rapture has me spinning
Has me dizzy
Has me grinning
While your capture has me seized
Has me high
Has me pleased
Choosing to stay as your prisoner of war
Hence through rapture and capture
It's you I adore

Give me a day
Give me a year
Give me a lifetime
Just give me a chance

Chapter Four

I wish I didn't love you
The way that I do

As I bask

As I bask in the ambiance of you
Absorbing the glow of your glory
Intrigued by the tale of your story
Joy cocoons me like a caterpillar
Your passion releases butterfly me
Flying on splendor
Splendidly lying beneath you
Underneath your shelter
Shielded from the chill of solitude
Lonely is a bitter friend
That loves my company
We've been cellmates so long
That it fights my hope
Running me towards the shelter of you
Gifting me with the presence of you
Creating an army of the you and me two
Such a magical number makes a duo
We can take on the world
With blind faith
Knowing that the way we feel is worth this trial
Never was an armor so strong
Nowhere is the shelter as real
How we shine in a sea of hollow hearts
Wishing they knew our answer
But our riddle is just for we two
Mapped by destiny
Planned by chemistry
What we have was blessed by the stars
And perfected by the heavens above
Birthed by harmony
In a frenzied state of need
Holding each other as refuge
From the infamous fury of solitude

Imperfect timing

Why now?
Just when I thought I was ready to greet the world
My preparedness has holes the shape of hearts
What now?
Is my plan supposed to adjust
For what could be mystique
For what could be lust
So when?
Will I be notified of the new directions at hand
I'm standing still, looking out
But you're not where I stand
I guess I'm still trying to find you
In the middle of finding myself
I don't feel as good about this as I once did
This histo' of love has wrecked me
Giving birth to new levels of pain
Seeming all but I are sane
How come?
The simple pleasure of rest
Has been ripped from my clutches
Though I fight the robbery
My dreams are paused
While I count thoughts of you
Hence the sheep get to sleep
I am forced to reach new heights in arithmetic
1001, 2002, I count and count these thoughts of you
Why me?
Something tells me I'm the only one sleepless
That I'm alone in the deepness of this single solitary
emotion
Why you?
Why is it that thoughts of you
Crowd my mind
And pump my heart

Memories of you
Have froze my time
And jumped my start
This wasn't a scheduled stop on my path
Though I am sure that it will be hardest to forget
So I will pull over and pause
But will you catch the cause
While I park and wait for you
Will you bring with you my new route?
Will you help to show me what love is about?
Will you ever show up?
It's oh so cold
It's oh so quiet
It's oh so lonely
It's oh so dark
Will you come to warm my soul?
Will you help my heart sing?
Will you come to keep my lonely company?
Will you light the rest of my days?
Will you?
Or is your heart set a day behind mine
Shall I wait?
Or is your heart set a day ahead of mine
Am I late?
If only I knew my way back
This detour has me scrambled
But I'm not concerned about the path ahead
For I know that your smile is on its course
Waiting to taunt me
To help lead the way
I know that you're out there
But will I see you today?
My compass is spinning your name
And drawing your face in the sky
Is that how you want me to see you, to die?
Just let it be said
And I shall paint the ground red
My blood only courses for you
So death will not pause my search

But allow me a new view
Looking down from my perch
Tracing your moves with mine
Feeling your heat from behind
Hoping that the chase will end
With both of us victors
Both of us high
Oh Damn!
I just remembered
It was my will to die
How now?
Will our togetherness ever see light?
I will cloud your day
I will cloak your night
At least I'll still have you in view
Yet, still you won't know
That my love was true
Because love showed up unannounced
And I don't know whether the timing was off
But I do know at its timing I scoff
While I wander the skies
Awaiting your demise
It's the only way
You'll ever see
The love that's in my eyes

My love

It's you my love
That has my heart singing in the tune of joy
Beating in synch with yours
I dance to a rhythm unheard by my ears
This beat thunders loud through my core
Making me always need you more

It's you my love
That has my smile brighter than the sun
Beaming from my soul
The rays of my light
Burn blazes across my field of fears
While drying all of my tears
I am happy's virgin
Aiming to please
Glee breaking me to the surrender of bliss
Hooked from our very first kiss

It's you my love
That has my mind making mazes
Trapping itself in the luscious lure of love
Stuck inside the promise of forever
For this love is never ending
Coursing forwards and backwards
Through and around time
Floating in a haze of peace
For in this love
We two are locked together
Grip stronger than we could have imagined
Or I could have dreamed
You see *Love* never liked me
Or so it seemed

It's you my love

That has my eyes working overtime
Drinking your image with a never ending thirst
This drought of joy plaguing my vision
Each time I blink
I see you for the first
Such a sight for a sore soul
Keeps me watching and wishing
Hoping and praying
Thinking and singing
Pleasing and playing
For in your eyes I am reborn
Brand new
Just for you
You found the key
And unlocked the hurt
That had made a home in me
Releasing a flood of desires and hopes
Washing over heartache's valleys and slopes

It's you my love
That has taken my future captive
Pushing past my gallant guards
Forcing misery back
Chasing pain away
Moving forward
With you, with me
Moving onward
Through us, through we
I am sunk in love
Swallowing your presence
Choking on my nerves
Needing to be near you
My skin itches for yours to scratch it
My mouth waits for yours to match it

For it is only you my love
That has awakened my inner volcano
Causing me to erupt with joy flowing like lava
Leaving my heartache in ashes

Let it burn as it passes
Because in your arms
I am alive
I am awake
I now tremble
I now quake

It is you my love
   -Only you that makes me this way
    -Only you my love
     -Just you my love
       -Forever us two my love

Chapter Five

You are all I see

Visionary

My lids are adorned with your image
My pupils are painted with your smile
Vision so clear
No matter how near
You
Are all
I see
Lash locked to lash
But I'm enthralled with my view
So happy that I welcome Braille
To trace your face
My nervous tips tickle
As perfect as ever
Though my eyes are left fickle
I shall never peek again
For my lids are awash with all I can handle
No sunlight, nor candle
Just my vision of you
Your smile, your style warms me
My guile, our file warns me
That surrender is only the beginning
Misery's white flag rose when I shut my eyes
Submitting to the power of your presence
Magic's mystical flag flies full mast
Signaling my vision's acquiescence
Blinded by bliss
Branded by blankly blatantly bold bravado
Darkness has never felt so secure
Lashes laced like stitches
Keep my hero in sight
With my destiny in scope
You
Are all
I see

But my eyes are on strike
Marching for you
Staring through me
Seeking your majesty
Never was my empty so full

Stuck on you

Like a broken record
My heart skips in place
I love you
I love you
I love you
I love you
I love you
It's stuck on you
Singing an unfamiliar song
Since you are my first
Can you hear it?
It blasts through my core
From my soul
Through me
Begging for you to move your needle
Pleading for me to finish my song acapella
Speaking straight at your spirit
Hoping that your heart can hear it
I love you
I love you
I love you
I love you
I love you
The only lyrics I know
Sing me into an amorous trance
The only lyrics I know
Send me into a lover's dance
In the throes of love
I find myself lost
Yet still on beat
I love you
I love you
I love you
I love you

I love you
You give my song meaning
Being my muse
Ascending the apex
Making me move
Singing your similar song
Supplying my soothe
Allowing my words an ear
Seducing my swoon
I dip when you dip
Entranced by our tune
I love you
I love you
I love you
I love you
I love you
I love you
I love you

Be good to me
And I'll be good to you

Just be good to me
And I'll be great to you

Chapter Six

I'm more afraid of love
Than I am of being alone

Phobic

I often wonder
Why at times I'm blue
When the sky is not
Dark cloudy abyss affecting my mood
The same for sunny days
That can't reverse this curse
It seems I'm stuck
When my mind is heavy
And my soul is light
My eyes seek shade
Even through the night
I often wonder what it is that they don't want me to see
Constant visions looking back
As I step outside of me
Pain from the start
Need a cane for my heart
It's crippled by fear
Left sour and tart
But why?
Why fear what I don't have
This fear has me strapped
Snared in a spider web
Spun from *Love's* trap
Very peculiar how the web halts your mind
Unable to see clearly
Because the heart blurs the eyes
Blind to the truth
Mind left impaired
Aorta in control
Body limp and scared
Could love walk in?
Is the door half open
Or is the door half closed
And which do I want it to be

If it's open, who is it?
If it's closed I did it!
Mute minds can leave your heart exposed
Why is it better to have loved?
When you can save yourself the pain
And save your heart the stain
But what am I saving it from?
Locked away so long
The key may not fit
Dead-lock bolted still
The bluer I get
Why me? Why now? Why me?
Did *Love's* clock tick
While I was stuck on tock
Maybe I'm love sick
Maybe it's love shock
Love's labyrinth has me afraid
Scared of losing myself in *Love's* ocean
No preserver of life
Just a victim of emotion
I'm drowning
I've drowned
I'm gone
Missing in action
Sorting out *Love's* faction
Will I ever see the light?
Bright it may be
This light I can't see
I'm blindfolded by fright
Trapped in *Love's* maze
Froze in its daze
Something tells me *Love's* found a way in
All exits are closed
All gateways disposed
My crafty opponent may win
Blue hues fading
Fears evading
Cloudy skies now turning clear
Sun exposing the new victim chosen

I feel that *Love* is here
Sneaking through, the feelings grew
I know now my heart it's near
Trapped inside
Nowhere to hide
This *Love* must battle my fear

Knock Knock

My heart's silence
Is being broken like plates at a Greek wedding
Opa!
I was oh so used to the quiet
There's someone at my door
Wrapped up in Cupid's violence
Who is it?
What do you want?
I'm scared of opening the door
I've never had a guest before
Though my heart is on "**E**"
My fuel is burning fast
They're still knocking
I see they are tenacious
But I'm not quite ready yet
Come back when the oceans are grass
And the rain turns to glass
Then I will let you in
The doorbell plays a melody for my soul
I don't think they heard
Because this is just absurd
I'm not dressed for company
They came unannounced
Who is it?
What do you want?
They're never going to leave
My heart's pinned on my sleeve
Why can't I take off this shirt?
The doorbell sings again
Now a serenade
My blood is rushing like the Nile
I'm excited, but why?
Come back when the Moon is the Sun
And Armageddon's begun

Then I'll be ready
They're still knocking
Who is it?
What do you want?
Why do I feel so open?
Gaping like Niagara
I'm falling face first
I know there's pain to come
Where are these feelings from?
Why are they turning the knob?
I'm not expecting you
Come back some other time
When the sands are turned to snow
And hell is the place to go
Who is it?
What do you want?
I still don't have a clue
How did we meet?
Or have we met?
Why are you still knocking?
What don't you get?
I'm not available right now
Come back when *Everest* is small
And the *Leaning Tower* falls
Then I'll be willing to visit
Knock Knock
Who's there?
Still no reply
Wait a minute I'm not quite ready
Come back when war fights truce
And right is obtuse
But I'm here now.
I know, but I want you to go
You can't see me like this
My heart is empty
My mind is on crazy
But I'm on time.
Though I'm not
Cupid and I are fighting right now

He thinks you're meant for me
But I don't seem to agree
Your timing stinks
Is this the right heart?
Probably so, but now you must go
I'm not prepared for you
I'm too scared of you
I'm not the one for you
Is this the right day?
Perhaps, but you can't stay
I wish you'd go away
I know that you're afraid.
Yet, my wish you still degrade
Come back when the mute can talk
And the great white can walk
Then I'll be ready
The doorbell plays a concerto
Who is it?
What do you want?
Why me?
Why now?
I can't take it anymore
I must go to the door
Out the hole I will peek
For my caller I will seek
You should have said it was you
Come in *Love*
Let me take your hat

Pain of Maybe

Damn!
This hurts
My mouth is full of answers
My mind is full of questions
My heart is full of you
I've fallen and can't get up
But I don't want to
For it's love that I'm falling through
Will my decent ever stop?
My eyes are closed
My ego exposed
I'm caught up in this drop
Anticipating hitting bottom
Will that mean the bottom of love?
Depends on your answer
For until you speak
I'll stay weak
While falling from above
The indigo in my heart
Is being chased away by persimmon
Cobalt hues, my thoughts, my blues
Now kissed by the sun
But behind the sun is the pain of maybe
Maybe you will
Maybe you won't
Maybe you do
Maybe you don't
Maybe is too much for me
It's driving me blind
I am shunning the light of the truth
For the darkness of my dreams
Where I control the reality
And I control how it seems
Though I know that when I wake
Control of your words I can't take

Hence it's the maybe that's piercing my soul
Digging deep into the middle of my hopes
Ripping a battle line
Through the yeses and the nopes'
Helplessly I sit
Feeling my massacre
Succumbing to the pain
What more can I do
But wait to see
If you love me
The way that I love you
I can sit here forever
Watching my murder
If that's what you want
Waiting to see which side of maybe you fall on
Either side, I'll be there to catch you
For either one last time in my arms
Or your eternal shield from all harms
Maybe
Maybe not
Who's to say?
You!

Chapter Seven

You are the only wonder
Of my life

T-N-T

As you near me
I become an erect wreck
Anxiously awaiting your touch
Nervously preparing your throne
The slightest collision
Of my skin with yours
And my implosions begin
One after another, after another, after another … …
Until my essence is shot into existence
You spark my T-N-T
With one glance, one look
Our explosions are more than atomic
When we collide
The Big Bang theory is revised
Since nothing can measure kismet

Lust without reason

When my mind takes a trip
And it's your kisses that I sip
My thirst for love is slowly quenched
Needing to taste your lips
Rubbing my hands on your hips
My hunger for lust has my mouth drenched
I have no reason to be hungry
When my heart is full of you
Though my passion at times erupts
Leaving an empty space
Inside of a crowded place
For my ecstasy can over flow
When just the thought of you
Makes me grow
Eternal estrus is the state of being
That seldom has be seeing
The truth or the proof of my longing
Though in the back of my mind
There's a symbol
There's a sign
Directing me to take your tongue's thronging
Lapping it up, Licking it down
Pushing you up, pulling me down
Our tango keeps us tangled
In a knitted knot
More heat than hot
Upside down forwards
Right side up backwards
A friction fumble
A standing stumble
Into a tasty tumble
All cautions crumble
While mated mouths mumble
Spoken spells, speaking tales
Wrestling wetter than wishing wells

Tickles to tackles
Suckles to shackles
Mutters and moans
Grunts and groans
Hoots and howls
Screams and scowls
Noises need not make music for the moment
When there is a present melody
Melting my machismo into a delta of desire
Though this fire rages on unchecked
For it is the dry season
When lust without reason
Boasts blazes that burn
Where we hunger
While we yearn
Scorched-

Let Love Lead

To you my love with thanks
I smile, You wink
We share, We think

How joy wears our name
While we speak love
Into anxious ears
Sharing secrets of sad and sultry days

Our hearts are in step
Beating a rhythm of passion and pride
Leaving us to dance, to kiss, to chance

Welcome to my life

Fall into my love

Let go and let me

Love us

Love we

Let love lead

Chapter Eight

It feels so good

Encore

When I close my eyes
Darkness is you
Eyes shut tight
But you're in sight
I wonder why
You are the H to my O
Liquid dreams taunting my slumber
Waking to hear your voice
Where are you?
Trapped in my fantasy
I've swallowed the key
The only way you're going
Is if you're coming with me
I have you
Morphed into my psyche
Like a childhood fear
Afraid to let go
I squeeze harder
Please don't leave
Your absence takes my breath
It's all that I have left
You've nabbed my heart
Though you make me whole
We are one
Enter-locked like Siamese
I love the way we tangle
Flesh to flesh
Our heat in Kelvin
This is good
To the last drop, I drink you
Forever wanting more
I can't be quenched
You try your hardest
This is insatiable
Salivating at the thought

Aroused by the touch
Invigorated when you smile
I inhaling, you exhaling
I breathe you
Oxygen obsolete
Those lips my medicine
Dose after dose
Doctors don't always know best
You heal me
Aches and pains
Now moans and groans
Making sweet melodies
As we play our favorite game
Competition is fierce
Battling to exhaustion
No victor declared
Round by round
Blow by blow
Taking turns submitting
We are champions
Always ready for war
Soldiers in constant salute
While minds are AWOL
Delirious from pleasure
Pistols full of lead
Together we shoot
No targets for aiming
Yet mission accomplished
Though this war is far from over
Infinite ammo, guns always ready
Death is the only pause
And still we fight
Souls playing chase amongst the clouds
Love eternal
Passion unlimited
Desire grows stronger
We perform for the gods
Our never ending show

Pillow Fight

Forehead to forehead
Whispered words wrestle with lips
Speaking promises and passions
In the dark of night
Speaking wishes and wants
In the heat of our heaven
Together we conjure the call of lust
Together we conquer the chores of love
The words that glow in the dark
Keep calm the fears that fight flat lines
Next to you the world disappears
Bedmates in this bed
Bond to battle
And battle to bond
No place is as safe
And dangerous at the same
Pillows place platoons in perfect position
For amorous ammo to fall from faces
Words mean more
When the Sun plays shy
Desires play coy
When the Sun stays high
Instinctive night vision allows eyes to see clear
Distinctive night rhythms allows hips to free steer
Afterglow's RSVP answered and anxious
Together we boast
With tongues we toast
An epic win to a messy war
Sweet nothings fill my clip
Loading my gun
As you regroup your cavalry
Pupil to Pupil
Lover's glances inquire and instruct
Frontlines mounted in wait
I love the way you call to me

Always needing seconds
Craving the taste of your ruckus
I detonate kisses
And eagerly await the melee

I was a proud mute
Until the first time pillow talk
Conjured me chatty

The world thanks you for giving
my
Tongue occupation

I thank you
For giving my voice an audience

Chapter Nine

I can't get you out of my head

Out of my head

It seems I have a permanent tenant
Because I can't get you out of my head
Ever since you fell into my bed
I've been vexed
You cloud my thoughts
You cloak my dreams
You shroud my wants
You overload my means
Will I ever be free again?
Do I want to be free again?
You are double parked
At the top of my brain
And the front of my heart
You are the best and worst tenant of all
Best because you make me feel flawless
Worst because you bring out all of my flaws
Before you I am naked
While wearing a three piece suit
I can't get you out of my head
Don't want you out of my head
Still need you in my bed
Your absence is all I dread
But you're keeping me crazy
And leaving my head hazy
What a beautiful chaos that cradles my conscience
It lulls me into sultry sleeplessness
My once hollow head is overflowing with you
Remembering the sullen days of being a desperate dunce
Can't get you out of my head
I don't want you out of my head
My loneliness now plays dead
An *Oscar* worthy act
Since the fear of you leaving
Is the fear worth believing

How long can this dream last?
Wishing we never had to wake
How long until this fear has passed?
The threat of lonely I need to shake
Can't get you out of my head
Won't let you out of my head
So long for this love I've plead
Now that I have you
I'm not sure of what to do
Truly blessed to have you
This I know is true
You've finally found me
Though I've been standing right here
Desire for me dumbfounds me
If you want me, make it clear
Can't get you out of my head
Won't have you out of my head
I need you more than I've said
From the moment I rise and open my eyes
My mind plays replays of our play
As I look to the skies where the love bird flies
The clouds and rays sway as display
Of the intricate dance that you and I perform
In the ballroom of my dome
Through the alleys of my think box
In my heart you have a home
Inside of your valley I find detox
I can't get you out of my head
Can't let you out of my head
One earth can't hold the tears that I've shed
Over you, because of you, just for you, in glee about you
My need to have you
Supersedes my need for air
You bombard my brain
Like Bush did Hussein
But this is not an unwelcome invasion
Your ammo is kisses, hugs, and persuasion
This war waged with my white flag in the air
My heart's been caged

Leaving my defenses weak and bare
Can't get you out of my head
Don't want you out of my head
I can't free you from my head
Because if I do, I'll again be blue
And then emptiness will surely take hold
No other hue, would allow you to get through
To comfort and console my soul
The days before your residence
Were tilted and scattered with evidence
Proving that your presence is more than necessary
To battle and rattle *Love's* adversary
Solitude is bitter, it hits below the belt
Lonely is no quitter, it love's its presence felt
Happiness eludes me
It's harder done than said
The bliss you bring salutes me
So please never leave my head

Imitated imaginations admired by Reality

My reality is numb
While admiring the imitated imaginations of us
That I have allowed to cloud my head
For the truth of the matter is still to be found
While I live in the falsehoods of which I drown
You could never be mine
Though I'm forever yours
In this walking dream we are one
Only divided by sleep
Though even through slumber you flush my mind deep
So lost in this fantasy am I
That if I were to awake to the truth I'd die
For reality is not answering my prayers
So I gleefully fall deeper into non-truths enjoying my
descent
I open my heart while closing my eyes
For the truth can be seen
Even in the imagination
I can't shake the sensation
Of the lonely joining me in bed each night
Waking me at dawn's first light
Still my eyes are vacant
For the truth is shunned away
So vibrant in this nowness
That you don't even know I'm dreaming
For this trick has consumed you too
The imagined is taking my kindness for weakness
While reality is confusing the game
Twisting my name
Without any aim
Pointing the blame
While searching for fame
My heart won't be tame
My brain is the same
These efforts were lame

Now dance in my flame
So lost in my imitations that I have erased the path to the truth
Reality is perpendicular to the imagined
Either side of the 90 degrees is a parable
For in reality I am in infinite longing
Through the imagined I am never truly whole
For the truth is always nagging my mental
Joy serum courses through my veins
Putting the red on pause
While my mind plays each scene over again
Every frame shown with more reverence than the next
No more tears to expose my fears
For in the imitated you chose me
Together we dance through life
Wrapped in heaven
Dressed in glee
Speaking love
Stomping on hell
Immune to the world
Lost in each other's gaze
We are missing
Not our lips, but our souls are kissing
Rubix is completed
Premonitions are defeated
In the imitated we are one
Hence reality scoffs
On envy it coughs
The imagined is winning the war
Reality needs my favor
For the imagined has again over stayed its welcome
I resist its campaign
Giving in to the imitated
For in the imagined the two of us are featured
Entwined like vines
We stretch up and down
Rhythmic beats help move the sheets
As ecstasy battles lust for control of the friction

Endless passion driving the conscience to infinite
explosions
No minds left to blow
So thoughts are being seized
Reality is nearing defeat
So again on its knees
To me it pleads
Begging me to choose
Which one I want to lose
But my thoughts belong to the visitor
For the imagined has pulled all the stops and tickled my
desire
The imitated has given me the path to completion
The two of us as one
For many moons
And repeats of the sun
In the imagined I am whole
Shared destiny has reversed my frown
My heart's no longer cold
Reality has surrendered
I feel I'm falling down
Falling without you
Even though I never let go
Sirens are announcing our love now
But their squelch is breaking my grip
I am free
I am without you
You are glowing in the distance
Marking where I yearn to be
Your brightness is blinding
That glow is invigorating
You are the sun

Wake up

Wake up

Perfect Mistake

Good morning Heartache
Where did you sleep last night?
Because I know it wasn't with me
For you were replaced by thee
However something doesn't feel right
Yet my slumber has never felt such peace
You're not mine
Though you shared my rest
I can see it in your eyes now
Even though you're sleeping
You belong to another
But every time I look at you
I wish the truth would disavow
And allow us to share this nowness forever
Last night I found my purpose
And it is to be one with you
However, right now we are three
Because you belong to thee
My skin tingles with thoughts of our togetherness
My heart now dipped in blue
Beating to the melody of the magic we made
Beneath the moon's eye
Now forever it will play our song
Since it will be all that I have left
Once you go back where you came from
I'll watch you leave from the window
But you are trapped in my core
And captured in my memory
Even though you hold my soul captive
I surrender my spirit with ease
Waiting for the day
That you return to reclaim your prize
For my bounty is more than you could carry home in one
night
Needing a lifetime to count your riches

But until then
From my bed you must wake
For I belong to Heartache
Please our memories don't take
My heart will swallow them as souvenirs
Simply parting gifts
From this perfect mistake

Victory

Beneath my skin
The taste of sin quakes me to my core
Forcing an eclipse between my longing and my lust
Entering a versus battle with my quencher
Saharan sands sweep, swirl and stand
Suggesting soiled secrets
Seep sorrow and sad
Since saying "So long"
I miss your caress
I crave your kiss
Now that you're near me
Tomorrow will have to wait
Because I'm lost in this moment
Trapped in this gaze
While the tips of your ten
Deliver quivers and shivers
Through my spine
Around my mind
Riding through my red river
The essence of our union
Creates ripples in my fantasy
Shaking myself into submission
For any position poised
Knots of knees
Showing the birds
Teaching the bees
Produce fiery friction
Fueling my addiction
Your attention drives me drunk
Pump my veins and flush the pain
That grew in your absence
Sobriety sours sanity
While my high helps heal harbored hurt
Face to face
Heart to heart
The rhythm of our love dance

Waltzes two steps across the ballroom of pleasure
Before retreat and recharge
So it can repeat while at large
In pursuit of promised passion
Ivory ink spills from the tip of my pen
Spelling victory for my opponent
Meaning that I don't win
For this was a dirty war
Ended on the floor
I call a rematch
Let's battle once more

I choose you

Above any other

For the rest of my days

I am yours

My vow is golden

I belong to you

Let's claim our joy

Be true

Share life

Blend bliss

Live love

Chapter Ten

You are my hunger

Nocturne

The look in your eyes is calling
My line isn't busy
I've seen this look before
I love what it has to say

I've answered now I'm stalling
This moment has me dizzy
My hunger I can't ignore
Here on the sand we shall lay

I'm ready and I'm not
My will now fights my loin
I want it and I don't
I'm all mixed up inside

Oh yes! You've found my spot
Our bodies now start to join
Maybe we will, maybe we won't
Watch the moon seduce the tide

Night creatures are our crowd
Their eyes fill me with shame
We should but we can't
What if we're not alone?

Sweet nothings oh so loud
I love how you say my name
Together a rhythmic pant
Love stick taunting and grown

In orbit from your kiss
Your touch sets me on fire
Tongues in love at war
Eyes are playing shy

Right now in total bliss
Consumed by my desire
I could not want you more
Our heat has made me high

If you take me I am gone
I am ripe and I am here
My yearning now is strong
I am scared but I am brave

I see the approaching dawn
I am safe when you are near
Let's not wait too long
I'm now ready to be your slave

Too fast, just take it slow
Entangled we are bound
The moon now lights the scene
Eyes now sneak a peek

For the moon we give a show
The tide has lost its sound
The beach is now serene
Explosions we still seek

Approaching is the thunder
But not from the air
I'm close, but not quite
And I know you're close too

I'm above and you're under
As one we'll get there
Almost day from night
Sword playing peek-a-boo

United we blast
Though our orbits are coming down
The stars begin to fade
The moon begins retreat

Drained at last
From a smile to a frown
Why must the sun invade
Close your eyes, make it repeat

Moonlit Monsoon

The silence of the moment is blaring
Eyes are useless as darkness prevails
Ears are busy, though at rest
Feel the calm as the thunder grows
The storm is approaching
Whispers screaming, hands now eyes
Silence breaks for hearts iambic
Each kiss a thunderclap
Shelter around, not necessary
Time to play in the rain
Hence, to quench thirsty souls
To drench dry dreams
The storm is moving faster
The wind delivers secrets
Each gust floating on fantasy
Gail force powered by truth
Secrets, fantasy, truth share a ménage
Between only two
The storm is calling
Howling its introduction
Embraces now a security and a need
Held past comfort, on to cozy
Finding laying position for maximum enjoyment
Sighs, echoes, begs and thanks
The moment speaks for itself
While tongues take to the task at hand
Desires swallowed, erotica inhaled
The storm is knocking
Tapping on the window, with infinite fingers
Drip- drop-drop-drip-drop drip-drip-drop
Pupils shocked my lightening
Observe pure passion in flight
Sighted long enough to blink
And approve of the scene
Darkness' return is welcomed warmly

For the pitch of black allows the soul to yearn
While the mind lets the body play
The storm has possession
Winds have control
Fingertips tap a symphony
Background music for keeping pace
Limbs tease, motions please, tensions ease
This is what the storm had in store
Planned, mapped out, no shortcuts
Straight to business
It's parked and sat to rest
Keeping the tangled in knots
Helping the free get got
The storm is satisfied
War in instrumental break
Minds in replay
Loins locking and loading
The battle will go on
 Until everyone has won
Fingers leave the glass
Melody over
Thunderclap on mute
Clouds reveal the night
The moon is still in tact

Love Spell

I feel as though I'm falling
Heart's echo calling
Heart's beat stalling
Who am I and what is this?

I'm lost now from found
My pulse the only sound
In love I am drowned
Who am I and what is this?

I've lost calm to pain
No hardship, no gain
Thoughts wild from sane
Who am I and what is this?

Once empty now deep
Inside love did creep
Eternal love to keep
Who am I and what is this?

Soul warm from cold
Arms ready to hold
Feelings loud and bold
Who am I and what is this?

Butterflies from still
Open is heart's seal
Torn now, can't heal
Who am I and what is this?

Trembles like the tide
Waves from deep inside
Emotions no longer hide
Who am I and what is this?

Dormant now erupts
Passions it corrupts
Fantasies stirred up
Who am I and what is this?

Opened forever more
Too late to close the door
Desires do not ignore
Who am I and what is this?

Missing is its name
Kissing is its game
Too strong to tame
Who am I and what is this?

Entwined we are twins
In the shadows of your sins
We are how it all begins
Who am I and what is this?

Lust

You make me hate to master my
bait

Your touch feels better than
mine

Chapter Eleven

You broke my heart
And only you can fix it

Deception River

Since our first handshake
I have drowned in your deception
Your smile made no exception
To the truth
That you are absent of truth
While I am flooded with proof
That I was a fool
To stay in your favor
Now I'm choking on my mordant misery
Gagging on our heartache history
Wishing I knew how to swim
Above the falsehoods
Over the grim
But I know that love will one day save me
Even though I can't quite tread through these sour days
I'm not exhausted from trying
I'm just tired of you lying

Broken

It started with your smile
I said "how do you do"
Loved your voice, felt your style
You liked me, I liked you too
That was the beginning of my end
Who knew that I would be broken?
Who knew that I could be broken?
You thought that I should be broken
So here I sit, standing in pieces
Bruised, scarred, shattered, and marred
I only wanted to be wanted
Now I'm taunted, now I'm haunted
All of my dreams flushed down the drain
All of my hope replaced with pain
Why did hurt choose me?
How could I let this be?
I'm not blind, but did not see
You'd be the beginning of my end
Who knew that I would be broken?
Who knew that I could be broken?
You thought that I should be broken
Show me a time machine and I will use it
Show me that smile again and I'll refuse it
It was my void that did me in
It was my happy you tried to end
But why me? Why me? Why me?
All I did was treat you right
All you did was lie and fight
Though stuck in hope, I tried and tried
Born taught to cope, I cried and cried
You were the beginning of my end
Who knew that I would be broken?
Who knew that I could be broken?
You thought that I should be broken
It wasn't all bad, it started off right

You weren't all mad, from start a true light
Saying all the right things
Making all the right moves
Speaking words my heart sings
Finding all the right groves
I thought you were the one
I was your moon, you were my sun
I thought we were the truth
I held the question, you held the proof
I feel so misguided, so mislead
I tried to hide it, showing joy instead
You were the beginning to my end
Who knew that I would be broken?
Who knew that I could be broken?
You thought that I should be broken
Now it's over and my heart can heal
Still left open, you shattered its seal
What can mend my shredded soul?
What can fill my spirit's hole?
Hope springs eternal, while hurt lasts the same
Love's bright inferno will burn through your fame
Broken I may be, though hopeful I will live
You could not take from me
All the love I have to give
It started with your smile
It ended with your frown
Still wishful as a child
You did not break me down
You tried your best to hurt me
You tried to crush my joy
Love will not desert me
Love does not destroy
I knew I would be mended
I knew I could be mended
You thought my joy had ended
I'm still smiling, happy – **Ha!**

Know it all

Me know what me have to do
To free meself from you
But can it be done?
Or again will me run?
Right back to your trap
Right back through your crap
Me dreamt of freedom
Me heard of solace
Me know what to do
To turn me heart from blue
But will me take to the task?
To remove me tattered mask
So you can see the true me
So me can truly be free
Me tasted love
Me wished for bliss
Me know what me must do
To me meself be true
But will me stay the course
And resist our cosmic force
Tis' a spell that me is under
Twas' me love that you did plunder
Me crave cured
Me heart hopes
Me know better

Chapter Twelve

I just wanted to be loved

As heat leaks the Sun

As heat leaks the Sun
I awake with the approaching dawn
Ready to greet the world
Not knowing if it's ready for me
Rejuvenated by its heat
I am reborn
Each ray dancing on my face
Tickling my awareness of the task to come
The birth child warming my soul
Each finger tapping gently on my spirit
Its light reaching my heart
My body bathed in its glow
Though I'm still lying down
Serenity's supple silent soliloquy
Spryly speaking sweet serenades
Softly slowly singing silently screaming
Screeching squealing sirens
Suggesting sanity sang Sun's song soprano
Shouting "Sit square, stand straight, set sail!"
But my boat is docked
Hence the call falls on deaf ears
For I am froze when my bed is big
No one there to turn my ignition
My mind in idle
My soul in neutral
My spirit in drive
My body in park
So I will lay here
Until the position is filled
Until the heat drinks the sun
And the sun is again spilled
Waiting … … … …

Love Limbo

I have me in limbo
       Wanting to know what's what
             Where does your heart want to be?

I am in limbo
       Looking to see which way
             Where does your heart want to go?

I live in limbo
       Searching to discover your wants
             For whom does your heart want to beat?

I wake up in limbo
       Wanting to know if it will be today
             Of practice has your heart had enough?

I exist in limbo
       Knowing that you are the only one
             What proof do I need you to see?

I'll stand here in limbo
       Patiently planning my victory party
             When we collide, dual missions in stride
                 Love limbo shall misplace me

Finale

Empty
The void that shrouds me
The space that crowds me
Empty
The way I need to be with you
How long I've yearned to be with you
Empty
Through the whole of my life I wish you to be
Co-captain of my life, I wish you to be
Empty
How I could love you better than any please see
How I would shield you through pain from many please
see
Empty
The pleasures I plot for you are real
My treasures just hot for you are real
Empty
So close your eyes and visualize the glee that waits for
you
Open your eyes, be mesmerized, it's me that waits for
you
Empty
A life so full, but still incomplete, it's you that's missing
Pause now holds love, I'm here in my seat, it's you
that's missing
Empty
Each time I sleep my pillow delivers me to you
With my last breath, I deliver my soul to you
Finally

Chapter Thirteen

Letting us go feels like suicide

Obsession

I may need rehab
For my addiction to you
I taste poison on your lips
      Feel passion in your hips
I sense deception in your words
      Hear attention in your wishes
I read infidelity in your eyes
      Ride to glory in your thighs
My obsession is stronger than me
I know that your love is false
Knew that our joy was fake
But I feel so alive in this play
Though this straight jacket itches
It makes my padded room a perfect fit
For these four walls are my four horsemen
      Guarding your gaze from my grasp
          Hiding my heart from your harm
              Saving my spirit from your spell
However, my memories are mine to keep
Even a world away from my fix
My high still keeps me twisted
This cemented grin keeps my cheeks numb
Ear to ear, I am now the joker
These straps are tight
I pretend they are your arms
If this is rehab, I shall call it home
So lost in this haze
You are trapped in here too
Cursed and blessed be the day that you dropped me off

This Wall

I need to find a way over you
Like a Mongol commander standing at the Great Wall
I'm not sure of what to do
Like a leaf in the autumn, I continue to fall

I'm standing at the base
All around me stares your face
This wall was designed to defeat me
The more I fall the more you mistreat me

I have to find a way over you
Like a Mongol warrior trying to breach the Great Wall
Of what to do I have no clue
The more I pursue, the more that you stall

What wall?
This wall
Who's wall?
Your wall
My wall
Our wall
This wall

From here... ...

It's from here that I peer
Looking out amongst the ruins of life
Searching and lurking
Through the pain, through the strife
Wondering how it all went so wrong
Pondering why it's taken so long
To figure out the truth
Though no wisdom from my tooth
I'm stuck in the muck of my reality
While lost in the magic of what seems
I am me
But who am I?
I can see
Not through my eye
It's from here that I peer
Looking out amongst the wishes of love
Hoping and praying
But no directions from above
I'm lost in my lonely
With thoughts of you only
If I am to be alone
Then the truth I don't want shown
For my illusions are a happier sight
Wrapped in your arms
This day, this night
It's from here that I peer
Tip toeing through the mistakes that I've made
Shuckling and jiving around the hopes that I've laid
To rest – In this test
One day I will have it all
But this day I will fall
Through the darkness that I fear
While I hide and choke this tear
For the pain
Oh the pain
Spells sorrow for tomorrow

Though today looms hollow
As the hole in my heart
Left open by your absence
Made deeper by my conscience
Knowing I've made wrong turns
Away from kisses
Into the burns
Following hisses
My heart spills spurns
So I'll sit here and peer, until my path is clear
Drawing you maps to my happiness

Damaged goods

Whoever takes me now
Will have to accept damaged goods
Because I was left in pieces
A poor pitiful pile of pieces
Remnants of a sated soul
Shreds of a marvelous man
Shards of a hopeful heart
I am damaged goods
Nearly beyond repair
I may be mended
By the right touch
Beneath the right light
Before the right eyes
Between righteous hands
Whoever takes to this task
Will become my savior
Because all of the King's horses
And all of the King's men
Could not put my pieces together again

Chapter Fourteen

Distance from you
Is necessary and agony

Reminisce

I miss you so much
That I often bite my bottom lip
In homage to your trademark kiss
In no way close to yours
But my memory shoots me back
To the last time that you held my face
With those two supple hands
And made me breathless
Shunning air
I inhaled as much of you as allowed
The life you breathed into me
Was ever lasting
Similar to the warmth of our embrace
You make me complete
I wish you were here
Before me now
So that I could bow
To your feet
To thank you for the surge you send
Through my core
Through my heart
Through my seduction
Through me
The memory of your smile
Is enough to send my libido into overdrive
Looking for new ways to calm itself
Until at last we are face to face again
Dazed by destiny
Staring into love

R.S.V.P.

My weeping whispers call to you
Begging for you to join my flesh with yours
The echo of the night is taunting my call
Suggesting that you can't hear me
Are you trying?
Your nearness brings closure
To the chasm of my longing
Your touch – Your smell – You
My dreams are of you
My nightmares are of you leaving my side
In our togetherness my soul is set afloat
While my hurt hibernates
Until my company is gone
I need you more than air
I crave you more than solace
I love you more than myself
Sad and true
You are my reason for waking
Hating sleep, for my eyes miss the sight of yours
You look into me and discover all of my secrets
Without saying a word
Mated pupils birth glee
Though mated mouths birth splendor
While speaking promises of a love divine
The weight of my heart
Has hampered my hurt
While supplying my strength
For when you are not by my side
Weakness can at times prevail
So that sadness can proceed
Your presence is at full request
Needing your sane to keep mine in check
Where did you come from?
And why don't you take me back there, away from my
lonely here?

I taste you when I smile
Hunger quenched from ear to ear
Needing to know that you need me too
Wishing that soon you'll be coming back
Hoping you show that you will end
My heavy heart's hiatus

Boomerang

If I let you go
And you return
Then it is said
That this is love
But I don't
Have the nerve
To give up this dream
From my center
I am yours
Ever since our eyes first met
Letting you go
Makes no sense
Would you return
To rekindle truth
And worship in love
With me
If I let you go
And you return
Then my dream
Comes true
You are the one
For me
Fear is strong
Flesh is weak
Freak is loose
You are the thunder
Through my heart
Afraid I stand
No master plan
To keep your hand
In mine
Bloodshot soul
Alive in heat
Singeing solitude
Frozen in love

If I let you go
And you return
The prophetess spoke
The truth
Sunrise, sunset
I merge with you
In spirit
In sweat
Insatiable
Oh so scared
Of letting go
I fight my pride
Boomerang takes flight
I witness, I hurt
If I let you go
And you return
Around and apart
We will turn
With open arms
I wait, I stand
If this is love
My core keeps cautious
Love can fade
After love's been made
While hearts are ready
To stake, to break
To bloom in the bounty
Of our promise
Spinning while turning
Towards our purpose
We are bound
To the call
That seduces romance
If I let you go
And you return
Passion plead my case
You are part of me
You live in me
You shine through me

Boomerang in chase
Target locked in sight
This dream
Is oh so real
Touching you
Kissing me
On Destiny's dance floor
Together we sway
Ever since your return
I dance with no music

Chapter Fifteen

What we are is forever

Shall we

Let's align our fears
       Together we can master love

Let us align our dreams
       Together we can conquer life

Let's align our hopes
       Together we can destroy doubt

Let us align our lives
       Together we can capture bliss

Let's align our quests
       Together we can become one

Let us align our loins
       Together we can explore lust

Let's align our eyes
       Together we can witness truth

Let us align our hearts
        Together we can define trust

Let's align our souls
        Together we can live in peace

Fever

My heart skips beats to stay in sync with yours
Speeding my soul and mind towards you
Unable to gain control
I crash!
I burn!
Fueled by love
My reality is inflamed with desire
No tears to kill this fire
My inferno rages on
Smoldering
Taking in its path
Any hopes to be sane again
My sanity ran the moment you rushed my conscience
Bogarting your way into my history
I am an open book
With empty pages
Being swallowed by your pursuit
My soul is waiting for the invasion to complete
While my mind struggles to comprehend
The fact that you chose me
Flanked by your fondness
My fear of love has flat lined
Hence, I believe we are forever

Child's Play

I know you are, but what am I?
Parables planning problems
Are provoking me to think
That my answers are lacking
The reasons I don't understand our plight
Evade me like the thieves of my heart
Running from my chase
Chasing away my hope
Hoping I won't lose
Losing all my faith
Am I?
I know you are
I'm watching from inside the gate
While your soldiers attack the border
Fighting to get in
I'm afraid of the invasion
I'm vulnerable
Inside I hold the truth
The soldiers want their prize
Like the Berlin, my wall is falling
What now?
My soldiers are traitors
Each siding with you
I'm left to fight alone
I'm left to fight in vain
I can't give in
Past the wall is a river of pain
Waiting to drown and swallow
All that tempts its tide
Unlike the wall
It flows from my tears
Each eye a delta
There's more where that came from
Won't you give up?
Swimming upstream, downriver

How long will you last?
For beyond my river
Is my forest
Each tree marks a notch on my heart
You love me, You love me not
Each leaf that falls is a promise of love lost
Each needle that pierces your sole
A glimpse into my hurt
Every fallen tree
A roadblock slowing your demise
Winners of the forest
Must cross my lake
My own ocean
Waters thick with the lies been spit
Good luck with that
No ocean floor
No fish
Just filled with every wish
Of love
Can't stay afloat when the spit is thick
Pulling you down
Keeping you under
Taking your control
Placing it in my grasp
But I don't want it
Too easy, keep fighting
Come out from the depths
Into my maze
Labyrinth of lies
One way in
No way out
Can you figure?
Think to how we began
You still think I'm worth it?
Every corner you turn
A memory of deceit
Each dead end you encounter
A reminder of the fact
That you are in a war

Laced by those before – You!
Just follow the signs
I'm pulling for you now
Go left – Take a left – Make a left – Another left
That's not right!
Step out and you'll see the answer
The way in, same as the way out – Lucky
That was a test
But not so fast
There's more to come
Hanging in there?
My mountain has replaced my lake
To the top you must go
If the prize is to be claimed
Every elevation is a step in the right direction
Showing your desire to win
You prove I'm worth it
From the top you must drop
Blind to the fate below
Will I catch you?
Is your battle over?
We shall see
While falling, count the ways that you love me
Run out of fingers?
Still got toes – Keep counting
Your fall is a journey
Back in time
Through the future
Around the present – In circles
Are you deliciously dizzy?
Or lusciously lost?
You're doing good, almost near the end
Now you must walk
Through these fires fueled by sin
Watch the flames dance to my desire
Keep up
But don't get caught up in their beauty
Because you won't see me
I'm more than that

But this will prove
Stride through my passions
And feel my heat
My inferno past boiling
I'm just on the other side
Still want your prize?
Cold to ice, but melting
As if you've been here before
Can you see me through the flames?
Look harder
I'm dancing in the snow
Chilled by my dreams
Dreams of a prize well earned and a nightmare spurned
Here I am, come get your prize
I've been here waiting
Waiting for you
What do you mean you got lost?
Look at the map
You've been in love the whole time
And so have I

Can?

Can we share
  A holy stare
    And gaze into
      Our love

Can we move
  Grind and grove
    And dance into
      Our love

Can we smile
  Be free, be wild
    And laugh about
      Our love

Can we glide
  Can we slip, can we slide
    And fall into
      Our love

Can we?

Chapter Sixteen

Give me your hand
I'll give you the moon

Give me your mind
I'll give you the Sun

Give me your heart
I'll give you the world

Three

When you spoke the words
"I love you"
My ears became the Grand Canyon
They echoed those three words
Until I could hear nothing more
Until I could understand nothing less
Those three words
Just those three words
And I was finally complete
I was completely whole
I was wholly fulfilled
Filled with glee
Gleefully deaf to the rest of the English language
Those three words
Those three tiny gigantic words
Set me free
And cuffed me to bliss
Shackled me to you for life
Your proud and pleased ball and chain
You belong to me
I belong to you
We belong as we
"Yes! I love you too"

Reborn

Our heat melts the tundra
Sending alabaster flows
Over the hills, beneath my toes
This union is boundless
But contained with two
Love so real
That my mind thumps itself
To keep up to the truth
That this is bliss eternal
An ever blazing inferno
This love has set my spirit ablaze
Let me burn in the flames of you
3rd degree is only the beginning
I wish to be the ashes of romance
That dance through the sky
Soaring past high
Landing in the heavens above
Together we battle lonely's brigade
In a bitter war to no end
For alone has the better record
Though we never give in
Defeat means disaster
For a love that soars through hope
Past wishes
Over and around prayers
Oneness with you seems to be my destiny
No other direction leads to you
Therefore I will run circles until dizzy
So that each time I'm lost
Finding you will be my rebirth
Over again and again

Chapter Seventeen

You make love real

Crooked

This feeling has me bent
Straight like a knotted tree
I've never felt this way before
My heart its own hymen
Broken by the words you speak
I inhale your vocals
No longer air I breathe
My heart beats like rain
Each drop its own rhythm
This feeling has me bent
Eyes that hate to blink
Afraid to lose sight
You may be a mirage
My desert's own oasis
Up and ready, yet untouched
That smile lights my darkness
Those eyes keep me awake
Your voice keeps me frozen
This feeling has me bent
A tongue without words
Verbiage replaced by moans
Possibilities causing fear
Fantasies creating fright
Nearness stirring growth below
Ready and willing
Flag at full salute
Breaths mute but loud
This feeling has me bent
Kissing the Pacific
Sahara taunting within
My geyser charging
My pulse climbing
My body melting
You send me up from down
Ready for my flight

I lay out as sacrifice
This feeling has me bent
Laying flat, pointing up
Eruptions of the Richter
Spent and wanting more
Your whisper echoes
My ears like sponges
Skin glistens with joy
Loins quiver with glee
Expectations surpassed
This feeling has me bent
Pointing towards the stars
No fingers used to aim
I beckon you once more
This I could share forever
Stay close for my survival
Your absence stops my blood
Death enters as you exit
Your entrance gives me life
This feeling has me bent

Frozen

I'm sitting and I'm thinking
My heart is now what's blinking
I close my eyes and I am with you
Dancing beneath the stardust
To the song of the night
Clutched in your warmth
Each star a twinkling light
Together we lose ourselves
Lost in the chorus of the stars
I crave only you
Fantasies frolic through my mind
For to be we were meant
Just for me, you were sent
Never let me go
Without you I am blank
My canvas waiting to be painted by your touch
Your caress brings me to life
Back from the black
Of a soloist's strife
I am reborn in your smile
Entranced through your desire
Enticed by your glow
With you I start and end
Frozen as you walk away

Epic love

Do you understand
This epic love
Can you understand
The call you feel
Can you understand
The cry you hear
Can you understand
How I need you
Do you understand
How much you mean
Can you understand
How deep I crave
Can you understand
How long I've yearned
Can you understand
How hard I pray
Do you understand
The force that leads
Can you understand
The way you heal
Can you understand
How long I'll wait
Can you understand
How strong I hope
Do you understand
Your infinite worth
Can you understand
The erotica caged
Can you understand
How perfect you are
Can you understand
How lucky are we
Do you understand
My journey is to you
Can you understand

This test is our quest
Can you understand
You are my brightness
Can you understand
You are my answer
Do you understand
Destiny is us
Can you understand
Eternity is ours
Can you understand
I am forever yours
Can you understand
That you are the truth
Do you understand
That this is real
Can you understand
My heart is yours
Can you understand
Your heart is my core
Can you understand
This epic love

Don't be afraid

For fear fights peace

Peace births love

Love orbits Utopia

I can take you there

We can call it home

Witness the dream come true

Chapter Eighteen

I can love you better

My love for you

My love for you looks down
Over gay Paris' tower
So tall, so high
Silencing the sun's power
Keeping heaven bright
No day, minus night
Just the light from my love for you
Oh the light
That glows through my love
My love for you
Overfills my heart
Like the Indian Ocean
Forced inside a bottle
Spilling over in a flood of devotion
With rolling waves of adoration
Foretelling of the love tsunami to come
Spinning tickle typhoons
That hunt, that run
Chasing behind happy hurricanes
With worshipping winds
And raunchy rains
My love for you blares louder that Krakatoa's hello
Crushing my inner ear
Hushing my inner fear
The echo of my taunting heartbeat
Sets the pace of our waltz
My love for you thunders
My love for you roars
My love for you thunders
My love for you soars
Up, over, around Neptune and back
And still it echoes
As it bellows, still it thunders
My love for you
Is a million page epic

Wrote and read in one night
A billion line love note
Born and bred by moon's light
Telling of the time
When love found its purpose
Speaking to the moment
Two souls became one
My love for you
Eclipses my love for myself
My love for my life
My love for true wealth
Leaving my lonely in total darkness
Leaving us in total oneness
Leaving me totally in love
My love for you
Drowns me in an abyss of bliss
I am immersed in love
In an abyss of bliss
I am submerged in love
In an abyss of bliss
I succumb to love
In an abyss of bliss
My love for you
My love for you
Oh, my love for you

Enabler

When I face you
It seems that you grin
So shy, so happy, yet so pure
With my eyes you uncover
With my eyes you uncoil
With my eyes you are you
Able to smile
Able to shine

When I hear you
It seems that you sing
So quiet, so muted, yet so loud
With my ears you are heard
With my ears you are music
With my ears you are you
Able to speak
Able to shout

When I hold you
It seems that you melt
So tough, so hard, yet so tender
With my arms you are free
With my arms you are safe
With my arms you are you
Able to breathe
Able to be

When I kiss you
It seems that you break
So straight, so scared, yet so brave
With my lips you escape
With my lips you explore
With my lips you are you
Able to feel
Able to find

When I merge you
It seems that you bloom
So kinky, so curious, yet so meek
With my body you are real
With my body you are relieved
With my body you are you
Able to lust
Able to learn

When I love you
It seems that you grow
So ready, so ripe, yet so true
With my heart you are found
With my heart you are bound
With my heart you are you
Able to live
Able to love

Chapter Nineteen

Let me love you

Acquiesce

I give myself to you
To do with as you please
My honor lies on your needs
Your joy - My quest
Your bliss - My aim
My heart beats in your chest
It's branded with your name

I give myself to you
To do with as you please
My honor beams from your smile
Your wish - My command
Your kiss - My prize
By your side I choose to stand
In my sight I want your eyes

I give myself to you
To do with as you please
My honor sings through your laugh
Your touch - My quiver
Your pleasure - My mission
Our embrace is love's illusive shiver
Tell me your fantasy, share your vision

I give myself to you
To do with as you please

You + Me

Come to me
In my arms is where you belong

Join with me
Siamese souls frolic on the moon

Feel through me
Dancing spirits kick to their own song

Rain on me
The dreams that make smiles in your slumber

Enjoy me
I am here to make happy the name of your fame

Seduce me
Craving to be animal in the shadows of the stars

Embrace me
Flesh to skin, valor with sin, your taboo touch tingles

Entrap me
My freedom's fantasy bows down to your rapture

Ignite me
Tangle free limbs, let's fall through the sun

Silence me
Lips locked in battle, leave me breathless

Stay near me
This union bombards my purpose with pride

Bloom in we
In your arms is where I belong

You keep me in chains

While I hold the key

Chapter Twenty

In love alone
Beneath shared sheets?

Motion Sickness

I woke up alone
But fell asleep with you
It shouldn't be this way
The stampede in my heart
Keeps me on your course
Wishing I knew a different route to love
You claimed I was number one
I always feel like number two
Your aroma steams my sheets
Your aura is in the air
Pillow talking Pinocchio
Filling my head with dreams of us
Shaking this bed with thrills and thrusts
I used to know the sound of the truth
Long before you licked my lobes
You used to taste like freedom
To this tongue trapped behind enemy lines
Fighting to free itself from lonely's hegemony
My bed has never felt so large
This crater from our cozy cuddle
Pulls me toward the vacancy
Left by your perfectly pleasing form
Leaving goose bumps to tease me
Allowing solitude to freeze me
Stuck on how you please me
And still I lay here alone
Going through the motions
Wondering when your warmth will return
To awaken my flat lined joy
To brighten my blackened dreams
To dampen my thirsty soul
Seems so easy for you to leave my side
I know you feel the magic we make
Though this is no trick
I find myself bamboozled by my beloved

In bountiful bereavement of our blessed bond
Begging you my baby to believe in bliss
I am yours for the taking
Smiles crowd my face
To chase away the frowns
Tears leave no trace
Inside my eyes so drown
I am soaked with you
While dripping my surrender across cold sheets
Laying on top of my white flag
In battle I stay stuck
While you look down from your fort
Making sure that I'm uneasy
Making sure that I'm not leaving
Making sure that I'm still grieving
And I want you still
The harder you fight
The stronger I feel
We shared a truce through the night
Together we laid in victory
Smiling while beguiling our bested battalions
Laying the red carpet down
So that lust and love could take their couple's stroll
Through our minds and down our spines
Sighs in silence
Seduce and suggest
That you are more mine than you show
Vows with violence
Detour and detest
My blindness to the truth that I know
Your game is hard to get
My game is easily had
This addiction is hard to quit
My obsession is making me mad
I'm crazy for you
Crazy
Sanity forgot me
The moment you called my name
My dreams stay in duress

There's no need to point the blame
I did this to myself
While watching you do it to me
So tired of waiting for happy to notice me
Then you noticed me first
But you keep me dead last
I can't say which is worse
Either my future or my past
I don't remember life before you
So happy for something
That I take all of your nothing
You'd rather take me for granted
Instead of not taking me at all
Perhaps I was born to be your fool
It's said that there are plenty of fish in the sea
What if I'm stuck in the Sahara
Waiting for love to rain down on me
Praying for love to wash away my hurt
Hoping for love to fall from you
Yet, my wait won't end
My prayers remain unanswered
Hope goes on endlessly
Because if you had a heart
You would see what you are doing to mine
Just looking for someone to call my own
Just trying to honor and cherish your throne
And still I lay here without you
Speaking this testimony to sunlit walls
In the same spot where we last shared the moon
Going through the motions
Sweating and vexed
Sorting last night's notions
Fretting and hexed
Fearing you will never come back
So here I shall lay
Until you promise
Until you stay
Knowing that my world is no longer mine
Believing that I am already yours

Waiting for you to claim your place in our cozy crater …

… … … … … … … … … … … … … … … … … … …
… … … … … … … … … … … … … … … … … … …
… … … … … … … … … … … … … … … … … … …
… … … … … … … … … … … … … … … … …

I smell coffee

Bliss Blizzard

Snow has graced the ground
But there are butterflies in my round
Hatched from the cocoon of my heart
Nervous ticks to nervous shocks
A loss of wits, my mental mocks
The coming storm has me snowed in
The coming storm has me snowed in
Tucked away, hidden from the approacher
Afraid of the wrath it rides
To my mind my heart confides
Sharing secrets I don't know myself
Drawing plans in silence, in stealth
Once again I'm the last to know
Though this time my blanket is snow
For the roar of the storm has me tucked in
For the roar of the storm has me tucked in
Snow has graced the ground
But there are bugs in my bed
Love bugs march until the bed bugs are dead
Ferociously eating my armor
Scratchy skin that itches for sin
Armor left thin as the love bugs win
The call of the storm has me shut in
The call of the storm has me shut in
The more I resist, the more the bugs eat
The more they persist, the more they defeat
My defense on the storm is failing
My offense to the truth is ailing
Exposure will be the cause
Of my death, of my pause
I don't have long to go
The storm chants through the snow
I am here and you can't win
I am here and you can't win
The deeper I seep

The harder I weep
For the love lice have now reached my flesh
But if they expose, my head to my toes
The truth will oppose
With its whistles and blows
Though I hide, I peek outside
Vanilla skies help paint the disguise
It changed the scene when it saw my eyes
But I know it's out there
I am here and you won't win
I am here and you won't win
Snow has graced the ground
Though my body is scorched by dry heat
It tingles from my scalp to my feet
My brigade is now bare
The love bugs have stripped me clean
Ignoring afraid, I am found serene
Bracing for the impact to come
It's coming to get me
There's nowhere to run
I've been hiding way too long
Can you feel me I'm in the wind
Can you feel me I'm in the wind
The earth is quaking
This bed is shaking
My fear's been faking
I knew all along that you were near
I felt all along that you were here
My soul heard you without my ear
What happens now?
Heart beats the answer in rhythm
A rain dance even though it's snowing
Our forecast stays love

Cold cozy

The thrill of love
Cancels out the chill of winter
I'm warm with thoughts of you
Thoughts of us
Though it's cold outside
My passion is like magma
Singeing my skin
From the outside in
Winter's chill fights strong
I am a blaze
Dreaming awake dreams of our splendor
Perfection takes notes from we
While goose bumps dance in fire
Tapping Morse code victories
Even though old man winter roars
Coughing avalanches of lust
Over the valleys a blistery blust'
But our heat is unmatched
Unchecked – Uncorked
Burning bright
Snowflakes avoid our orbit
For their defeat is eminent
Our triumph is promised
Still the wind stays froze

Chapter Twenty-one

You left my heart
Flat Lined

Paradise Lost

I lost my blue paradise
When I lost you
My skies fell gray
Whence they used to be blue
Do you know my dreams are owned by you?
My days are dedicated to remembering your smile
I am alive when my heart pumps your name
Thankful to choose you as mine
I drape myself with thoughts of you
Memories flood as misery goes
Dreaming of us is all I do
In promise my love for you grows
You are my shining star
My night sky is blessed by your glow
I feel you, even though you're far
You feel me too, this I know
How do I show you our purpose?
How do I show you my prayer?
How do I prove we deserve this?
You should feel that I care
Together is how we belong
Together is how we should be
The future is always unknown
Right now just think you & me

Wondering what to think

I am blank
While wallowing, wondering
Where, when, why, we went wrong
Whoa!
Woe is me
Do you have the answers?
Yesterday our tomorrow seemed so bright
Where did this darkness come from?
This lucid lunge at love is lacking light
What happened?
Our eyes shared a promise
Now our hearts share a problem
I fault you
Because I think you knew
That your heart wasn't true
When you said "I love you"
But you don't and you won't
I see the truth
Even though my eyes are shut
Realities raining
Relentlessly raging
Dreams of you
While wondering what to think

Royal Request

I'm so blue
Completely white outside
Sadness wears my face
Longing to be held, to hold
Wanting you to be mine
Wishing me to be yours
Remembering the laughs we last shared
Reminiscing on the glance we last stared
Old man winter rains white
Snowflakes give ballet through the sky
Mimicking our kisses
Snowmen blend just like you and I
Stacking up like wishes
To have you would make every birthday candle
worthwhile
To have me would be your own genie waiting for
direction
Treasures unlimited
You'll never have to ask
Just take my hand
Come take my love
Please take my blue

Twisted Happiness

It is a twisted happiness
That keeps me calling you
It is this twisted happiness
That sings me sad and beats me blue
It is our twisted happiness
That leaves my head and my heart
In a tailspin apart
Twin twisters, wicked sisters
Fighting each other for control of my chaos
Oh it hurts so good
My delicious pain lets me know I'm alive
The joy, the rain helps me feel I'm here
Running to you
Is like running with scissors aimed at my core
I'm afraid of falling
Though I run without looking
I continue to crave more
Of your threat
Of your killer kisses
Even though I know I'm going to fall heart first
I can't control my thirst
For the venom that you blow my way
For the poisoned promises
That you speak
That you say
But I'm so happy to have you
Vexed that you have me
My twisted happiness keeps me guilty and grinning
I stay sad happy, while you stay winning

Chapter Twenty-two

Until my last breath
I will wait for you

The Waiting Room

The moment that your eyes met mine
My eyes were no longer portals
You saw through me and drove me blind
So blind that my vision of you was enough
To keep my ebon days brighter than the Sun's glow
So bright that darkness had no meaning
Even though sight seemed so necessary before
I was born to do without vision
Once I saw you
The moment that your hand touched mine
My physical form became useless
Your hand incited my spirit to take flight above my flesh
So that I could stay cuffed to you
Clutched by you
Crushed over you
Could my hand find a better reason for being?
The spark that electrocuted my fingers
Waved through me on an unvolted current
Our electricity could power this universe and the next
The very moment that your kiss captured me
My life was no longer mine
Your lips sent a surge through me
That overloaded my senses to the brink of epilepsy
But this seizure was warmly welcomed
Never in my days had life been so live
Ever since we met you have never left my brain
Etched forever on my heart
So here I stand
        Waiting for the season that you surrender
            Waiting for the day that you return
        Waiting for the dawn that you acquiesce
    Waiting for the moment that you remember
        Waiting for the dusk that you relinquish
        Waiting for the hour that you are ready

Waiting for the minute that you maroon
Waiting for the second that you decide

Waiting... ...

Waiting for you

Waiting... ... ...

Waiting on you

Waiting... ... ...

I'm here waiting in the room where our souls mated

Waiting ... ...
...

Just for you

First love

First love
You have walked in and out of my life
Like sunbeams blasting through a dense fog
Always there but diluted
Not stifled but muted
Unequipped to stake your claim on endless love
You keep quiet
I listen hard
And the love that is
Must stand dry in our oasis
Waiting
To quench
Still it stands

How does it make you feel
To know that you are my
inspiration?

Truth be told
If it weren't for the promise of
our
Second coming-
I would never want to wake

Choosing instead to lay
In a curious coma
Waiting for your kiss to end
My sensual, intentional slumber

Chapter Twenty-three

We have unfinished business

Love you still

If I could keep you captive
Love would make your cell
Only kisses make keys
Vowing to be yours forever more
Eternity is too limited for me to prove
You are the reason I was born
Our love is the reason that I wake
Unity with you ignites me, excites me, decides me
Something in the way you look at me
Thrills me so that I tingle all over
Intrigues me so that I tickle inside
Leaving me thirsty for your wishes
Leaves me breathless, while gasping for you

Pretty Please

Come back to me my love
My life's just no good without you
My nights are so cold without you
My days are so dark without you

Come back to me my love
Since you left my heart has stalled
When you left my dreams were mauled
After you left, just your name I've called

Come back for me my love
Did you forget me when you left?
How could you forget me when you left?
Heartache found me when you left

Come back for me my love
I'm still standing where we stood
I can feel you where we stood
I can smell you where you stood

Come back into my love
For you my heart's still open
Since you my heart's still broken
Because of you, my heart's a token

Come back into my love
Just for you my love is waiting
For your eyes my eyes are waiting
On your touch my skin is waiting

Come back into my love
Come back for me my love
Come back to me my love
Pretty Please

Tick – tock – Tock – tick

Tick – Tock – Tick - Tock
We have unfinished business
Work still to be done like Mt. Rushmore
Our faces make traces over this open ended contract
And it is this fact
That stops me from letting go
That stops me from moving on
That stops my next assignment from its staggered start
Because the truth of my heart
Says that no other contracts can be fulfilled
Until our love is distilled
And has blossomed into its purest glory
Telling our beloved story
Of the time two hearts were stuck on pause
Because of unfinished business
Left to wither in time
Left to begin again, better than the first
Since our clocks were set by
One Sun, nine moons, and six stars
Ticking together, tocking' apart
When you return, it'll be my turn to leave
So I can reset my clock
While resetting my mind
Taking with me my end of this two-sided monster of a pact
With you here and me there
Maybe you will feel the need
To rush, to run, to speed
Back to my pendulum
Back towards my two hands
Even with one shorter than the other
My grasp is perfect
Patiently ticking and tocking'
While clicking and clocking the pace of your approach
Even though I never lost sight of you
Sight of my destined hour

Sight of my lover
Sight of my friend
Big Ben speaks spells and lies
Shading hell through the skies
We have unfinished business
With no expiration date
No start nor end time
Just the desperation to wait
With this heart on this chime
Though I keep staring at my watch
Wishing for the wizardry of a witch
To spin a root over our route
So that we could cross paths, while blending passions
With the promise of a contract carried out
With the notice of two clocks chiming the same time
Announcing perfection accomplished and destiny fulfilled
Pendulums in sync
Four hands locked to each other
To never let go again
So that our business can be complete at last
Though until that day, my hands shall stay stuck
Because even a broken clock is correct twice daily
Your move now
Tock – Tick
Tock – Tick

Chapter Twenty-four

My heart says wait no more

Hustler

You felt the need to lie
When you said you would be back
I fed the need to believe
To my arms you would run back
Now years of tears tangled with talk
Leave me wishing I knew myself better
Because I'd never met my masochist
Until you-
Pushing lemons into fresh wounds
Loving you has burned beneath it all
But it was those eyes that convicted me to you
My Blue Paradise
Azul heaven that cradled me with smiles
Indigo prison that shackled me with wiles
Cobalt coffin where I bit my tongue to death
Now I'm spent, now I'm left
And I can't share this dream alone
I was yours and I was waiting
You were right but you were wrong
I've been here anticipating
Held this place where you belong
This was over before it began
But lying to myself fed my fight
I finally held an army
To aid my assault on misery
You and I together ruled the world with matching
crowns
Anything between us was sacred and secret at the same
Everything between we was tainted and tasty like the
game
I wonder what my waiting has cost
Has my soul mate came and went
Why is my aim so loose and lost?
Lover's *Love Jones* leave me bent
I wish I could claim my time you'd wasted
But I would love you all over again with pride

My lie claims that I am not devastated
My truth claims that I'm best by your side
I fed the need to believe
To my bed you would return
Where we hungered
How we yearned
Finding the truths of the sensations we crave
Locating love laws, while we misbehave
Learning each other like our A'B'C's
Teaching each other to love, to please
Freaky frisky friction framed free friends for fun, for
frills
Tricky traction tricked and tripped trained troops trying
to tryst triumphant
We made fun
While love made us
Yet, still I am left
Gazing at clocks
Dazed by doorways
With wishful eyes
Making mirages of my missed lover
While making excuses for you
Though your truancy is proof
That I loved aloof
As you hustled my heart away
The longer I've waited
The clearer the truth
This was just a game
Play for your jollies
My heart you've invaded
Dishonest, uncouth
When you called my name
Played the fool of your follies
Blindsided by the glare of lonely
I walked hand in hand with my oppressor
Set and sprung my own trap
Releasing my gallant guillotine
I am left a headless romantic
With a heart still beating our song

Butterfly Flight

I changed myself for you
Held up in my bubble
Hid tight behind my barricade
My metamorphosis manifested by your call
Cocooned in caution
My fears you fluttered and freed
Lonely's larvae, I laid leery of love

I changed myself for you
Before my time
Before my prime
Hatched wholeheartedly
With out-stretched wings
Reaching for you
Taking flight through your shine
Soaring with you, for you, to you
Floating away from fear
Gliding and grinning in sync

I changed myself for you
Steadfast skeptic
Now a full fledged believer
Hollow-hearted hero
Becomes heartache deceiver
All at once I became lovable
That instance I was known gullible
Wings flapping to you
Heart hoping for truth

I changed myself for you
Used to the role of misery's martyr
My coy cocoon kept me captive
Once assigned to you
I resigned from my blue
Allowing my happy to be active
Butterfly wings flapping love's lively tune
Butterfly skies of the sun, beneath the moon
The lyrics of your love gave me flight

I changed myself for you
What have you done for me?

I changed myself for you
What have you done to me?

Was it your intention to leave my heart
my heart
In dissension
Or were you loving for sport?

Chapter Twenty-five

What's done is done

Love Hunt

The emotions that flush my form
As I write these words
Ring softly through my core
Nice notions flood my ink and pen
Memories of love no more
This is bitter sweet
Who knew that goodbye could crush my diamond pride
But I knew my heart would feel I'd lied
Once I said that I was fine
I felt my hurt scream loud from inside
Once confessed that you weren't mine
Is it really better to have loved?
I was just
Before you crossed my path
Like a black cat
You changed my fortune
My coffers were neat and bare before you
Now care, caution, and passion ring true
I look back to see you framed in my view
Wishing I had turned away from your gaze
Wishing I had studied more of your ways
Wishing you weren't part of my favorite days
Wishing your heart meant the words your mouth prays
Wishing your hoax was a temporary daze
Wishing my head was free of love's haze
Wishing my hurt had seen all of its plays
Wishing my soul would shake you as it sways
Wishing my heart had less tatters and frays
Wishing my name was not one of your lays
Wishing it was my heart that straggles and strays
Wishing you the best
As I close and end my quest
For this love hunt has left the hunter the hunted
Making this love hunt my first and my last

Holly's Help

High while huddled with Holly
The truth swam through her voice
Lapping proudly around my lovelorn confession
She spoke of the mourn of love
How its loss resembles death
Reality erased my grimaced grin
The truth bit me in my visions
Making me truly understand what it takes
To move on
I must mourn the love that was born
And bury the dream that once was
Ashes to ashes
Dust to dust
May our love rest and rue
Through peace means little as the truth burns through
Love's eulogy I must pronounce
I have to leave it here
I have to make it clear
That this love I must denounce
Now burial is the only resort
Grief blooms bold
Heart falls cold
Now memories of love I distort
We are no longer we
I am left, only me
Standing
My shovel-my crutch
My loss

Farewell
First Love

Contact: LoveDrunkBook@gmail.com

Bonus

Pieces from the forthcoming release:

"Love Hangover"

Choose again

Choose again
I beg you
There's no way
My love could lose
Consider what you are saying
Think of who you're slaying
With these wicked words
Chose again
I beg you
Are you sure about your choice
I never thought I'd lose
Repeat what you are saying
I hope and pray you're playing
With these wicked words
Choose again
I beg you
Can't you recall that night
Never thought my hand you'd lose
Do you hear what you are saying
Now it's our love you're delaying
With these wicked words
Choose again
I beg you
There's no way
My love should lose

I ain't got no more

It's all depleted
Your fall defeated
I am standing tall
Making sure your call
Falls flat with your crawl
Because it's hard for you to see
Not easy for me to free
The truth that I've hidden
From me
But the real is this
No hugs
No kiss
This is our time to part
I'm for real please know
Time to break, time to go
And find your home my door
I'm finished
Can't hold it
I ain't got no more
Well has fell dry
You flip flop, you lie
And the love I held
Is gone
The love you played
Is pawn
Your face is now my pain
I wish you well
We tried
You FAIL
And I ain't got no more

How can I lose the love I never had?

"Look's like another love T.K.O"
I'm flat on my back
While reality whoops my ass
Takes no sass
Since the truth
Leaves me 1
And you somewhere – Over there
How can I lose your love
When you never called it mine
I always knew what was
You knew you had my mind
Now I can't even reach the ropes
Stuck feeling my heart's rape
Wondering how I got here
If we never were there
I'm flat on my back
And what's real kicks my core
Only dummies give away love
In exchange for laughs-
Then a dumbass I be
Cause' the love I never had
Completely had me

www.ingramcontent.com/pod-product-compliance
Lightning Source LLC
Chambersburg PA
CBHW032119040426
42449CB00005B/193